A Walk On The Dark Side

The Dark History, Legends,
And Folklore Behind
The Haunted Vicksburg Ghost Tours

By Morgan Gates

Table of Content

THE TIME OF THE GREAT DYING
Chapter 1

Long before the Civil War, long before Vicksburg's founder, the Rev. Newitt Vick, came with his family to Mississippi Territory, before the first American settlers descended the Mississippi with dreams of a new life on a promising frontier, and before even the French and British colonist called this area home, these fertile lands along the lower Mississippi were home to Native American civilizations. Today, just 36 miles NW of Vicksburg lies an UNSECO World Heritage Site named Poverty Point. When Solomon sat on the throne of Israel, it was one of the largest trading centers in North America. By the time the Vikings began raiding England, the Mississippians Culture was well established in this area. Their civilization extended from the Gulf Coast up the Mississippi, well into what today is called the Midwest.

The Mississippians were no mere band of hunters-gatherers. They were an advanced civilization with organized government, extensive trade routes and public works projects, in this case **large earthen mounds**. Emerald Mound, just over 50 miles south of Vicksburg, is so large a game of football could easily be played atop it. Even their small villages featured central mounds large enough that a small house could be located on one. This county is dotted with those village mounds to this day.

The first European explorer to have contact with this civilization was Hernado deSoto. His writings described many towns of several hundred people or more, surrounded by cornfields and orchards. These towns were seldom more than a day's ride—15 to 20 miles— apart[1].

Peoples of the New World had never before seen such a cavalcade of strange men and even stranger animals. DeSoto's first impression is truly Shock and Awe. However, his high-handed, disdainful methods were his eventual undoing. Fear of his mounted tactics and armament sustained his mission, but by the time he reached the Mississippi, word had spread ahead of him and he was met with armed resistance. Many of his men and much of his equipment were lost to raids and combat. Disease and exposure thinned his ranks even more.

DeSoto died of disease, probably somewhere around modern Ferriday, LA. The few survivors of his expedition were able to cobble together some crude boats and begin their escape down the Mississippi River, but they were hounded almost all the way to the Gulf by large war canoes filled with dozens of warriors. We certainly know they used such vessels, so it is likely that these warriors were in fact the Mississippians. Several years later, a ragged handful of survivors straggled into Mexico City with their tale of death and destruction! No further expeditions were launched into this dangerous and unprofitable area of the world.

There is no written record of what happened in this area for around 140 years or so, but with a bit of extrapolation we can come up with a reasonable scenario. We know infectious disease was common in the dirty crowded cities of

---

[1] De Soto's secretary, Rodrigo Ranjel, kept a dairy, which has been lost, but apparently was used by Gonzalo Fernández de Oviedo y Valdés in writing his La historia general y natural de las Indias. Oviedo died in 1557, but the part of his work containing Ranjel's diary was not published until 1851. An English translation of Ranjel's report was published in 1904.

Europe. Smallpox had been present for at least 1,000 years at the time of deSoto's expedition. It was such a common disease that there was probably not a European alive by the 16th Century that had not been exposed. It was still a deadly disease, but a certain amount of racial immunity had built up. It is not unreasonable to suppose that one of the members of deSoto's expedition brought this virus—and most likely others such as influenza—and unwittingly deposited it in the virgin soil of the New World Indians. It probably spread along the trade routes, slowly at first, but then it began to pick up speed. Soon it was raging like a wildfire in that tinder-dry forest of unprotected souls.

Researchers [2] speculate that serious communicable disease, with the possible exception of syphilis, was pretty much unknown to pre-Columbian Native Americans. How long did it take for the first case to reach the Mississippians? … A month? … A year? … A decade? What did they think was happening? …The wrath of the gods? …The end of the world?

The shamans were as helpless as everyone else. They too sickened and died. Whole families died, whole villages died. According to local folklore, the Yazoo River, a tributary of the Mississippi River just north of the city, is said to translate to mean "River of Death" (In truth, this can be said of many southern rivers with Native American names). As bodies stacked up with not enough healthy people left to dispose of the dead, were the bodies flung into the river? Nobody knows!

---

[2] Charles C. Mann, <u>1491 New Revelations of the Americas before Columbus</u> Vintage E-books

Societies collapsed, but in time the population stabilized at a much lower level than before. The remnants of other tribes took in the survivors. Society reorganized on a smaller scale and different tribes migrated into the area.

Without a written history, and with the death of those who passed on the oral traditions, the time of the great dying slowly vanished from living memory.

The Mississippians were gone, and only their mounds remain as mute testimony to their presence here on earth.

In the intervening generations, smaller, less well organized tribes inhabited the land along the river. The Yazoo tribe became one of the larger and more established tribes in this region. Then in 1682, the light of Western history was again to shine on the lower Mississippi Valley. *René-Robert Cavelier Sieur de La Salle*, better known in American textbooks as just Robert LaSalle, descended the Mississippi and claimed the entire Lower Mississippi Valley for France and this area became part of the French colony known as "La Louisiane". In 1698 French Jesuit missionaries establish an outpost along the Yazoo River, a few miles north of modern Vicksburg, to minister to these people. In 1719 the French military took over the outpost and it became Fort Saint Pierre. By this time a small surrounding community known as Yazoo Post had grown up around it.

The French had established several of these outposts along the river, as well as plantations, and attempted to compete with their British rivals by producing tobacco. The nearest to

Fort St. Pierre was Fort Rosalie, about 100 miles downriver. There, demands for land by the French, angered the local Natchez Indian tribe and in 1729 they massacred the inhabitants of that outpost. Shortly thereafter, the Yazoo followed the lead of the Natchez tribe, and massacred the inhabitants of Fort St. Pierre. The French government, in retaliation, essentially wiped both tribes from the face of the earth. **Is it any wonder that restless spirits must have wandered these hills long before Vicksburg was founded?**

THE HIGHWAYMAN

Chapter 2

The Natchez Trace was a road through the wilderness that predates European settlement in the lower Mississippi Valley, perhaps even human habitation. Science now tells us it may have started as a trail made by buffalo as they migrated to salt licks around Nashville. In the late 18th century, the first white settlers pushed across the Appalachian Mountains into what today is Tennessee, Kentucky and Ohio. They found rich farmlands that produced abundant farm surpluses, but it was hardly feasible to try to retrace their steps through the mountain passes in heavily laden farm wagons. Instead of going up the mountains, they went down the rivers—down the Cumberland or the Tennessee—into the Ohio and from there into the Mississippi.

A cottage industry arose building flatboats, which are simply shallow drafted wooden barges. Flatboats loaded with corn and salt pork, or even live hogs, would drift slowly along with the current on their one-way trip out of the wilderness down to the then Spanish cities of Natchez or New Orleans. Spanish gold and silver spent just as well as any other! The long, slow journey was fraught with danger and could take a month or more. Upon arrival at Natchez the farm products were sold. The flatboat was then disassembled and sold for scrap. Some of the profit was likely spent on recreation at "Natchez Under-the-Hill" a place well known for drinking, gambling and prostitution. Then the long walk home began.

These Kain'tucks, as they were called, were a hard lot. A

large, broad dagger, known as an Arkansas Toothpick, in their belts and a squirrel rifle over the shoulder would not have been uncommon. But the pouches of gold and silver they carried were too great a temptation. Thus, bands of highwaymen or outlaws, heavily armed and ruthless, were common along this wilderness road.

At the time, this area was under the de facto control of Spain. This area had flown many flags in the 80 or so years that Europeans had called this part of the world home. France established Fort Rosalie in 1716, which later became Natchez. Britain took control after the French and Indian war. (A true world war that was known as the 7 Years War in Europe.) Spain seized it toward the end of the American Revolution. In 1783, The Treaty of Paris, which ended the American Revolution, awarded it to the fledgling United States, but the Spanish were not consulted. That required a separate treaty concluded in San Lorenzo, Spain in 1795.

Here, that treaty was known as Pinckney's Treaty. It recognized the Western boundary of the United States as the Mississippi River and the southern boundary as the 31st parallel, but therein lies the rub. The 31st parallel, we know today, is about 100 miles south of present day Vicksburg, but geographic location then was not the precise science it is today. Spain claimed it lay just about where the northern city limits of our fair city lay today, and they had a fort and a garrison there to enforce that point of view. The land did not come under U.S. control until sometime in 1798.

The remoteness from civilization and confusion over who was in charge allowed the highwaymen to operate with near impunity! Potential witnesses were not often left alive, and even if they escaped with their lives, how could one prove their case against such shadowy figures? Rewards and bribes were often more effective than regular law enforcement as we know it today. At this point in time is when a nefarious character, a man by the name of Andrew Glass, steps out of the shadows of the past and into the light of our story. Not much is known of this man's past as we might well surmise, but apparently, he had built a reputation for himself among the rogue's gallery of the Trace, for at some point the Spanish authorities offered to buy him off!

A common misconception among the law-abiding is that men turn to crime out of desperation, because they have no other option. But the truth, in many cases, is that it is simply the nature of the beast!

Andrew Glass was offered a sizable Spanish land grant just to the southeast of the Spanish fort at *Nogales*, better known in English as "The Walnut Hills".

Land was money in those days. In fact, it still is today. It was believed that once Andrew Glass became landed gentry his depredations along the Natchez Trace would cease. Perhaps Mr. Glass did have aspirations for a better life, for he accepted their bribe and took possession of the land. He chose a spot just over a mile east of the river near a stream at the bottom of a large wooded hill. There he built a small two-story house of locally fired clay bricks—just two rooms, a bedroom up and a general-purpose room down. Still thinking like a robber perhaps, the upstairs was accessible only by a rope ladder that could be pulled up at night, and a log palisade surrounded the house. By some accounts, it was an Indian trading post, by others a tavern. Likely it was both, and like any well-established gentleman, Andrew soon took a wife.

Perhaps this settled life was not a good fit to a man accustomed to the adrenaline rush of the hunt and kill. Or perhaps the lure of shining gold and silver coin plodding slowly north so near at hand (The house is only about 16 miles, as the crow flies, from the Natchez Trace, a good day's walk in those days.) was just too much to resist. Andrew Glass soon returned to the Natchez Trace to pick up his old profession, but he had not abandoned the little house at the bottom of the hill. There is nothing better than a soft bed and a warm woman to return to after a couple of days' outing in the woods. Greed has been the undoing of better men than Andrew Glass.

Perhaps through a liquor-loosened tongue or through a paid informant—it matters not—word soon reached the authorities that Glass was up to his old tricks again. The Spanish Colonial Government that sent Methodist ministers to the silver mines of Mexico for preaching the Protestant creed (see chapter 3) was not likely to give a cutthroat like Glass a second chance. The next time a particularly rich party of farmers is headed north, an ambush was set up. A heavily armed squad of Spanish soldiers shadowed it up the Trace. When Glass and his band of bushwhackers attacked, they found themselves under the guns and steel of disciplined military men. Miranda rights and due process were centuries in the future, so most of the gang were quickly killed or captured. Glass was wounded but, in the confusion, he managed to escape.

While the nature of his wounds is unknown, we can make some reasonable assumptions. Had he been close enough to be slashed by a saber or run through with a pike, he probably wouldn't have escaped. So, let us assume a musket shot perhaps as he was running away. Discretion is the better part of valor after all.

Spanish muskets of the day were large bore. 50 caliber and up were the norm, and they were likely loaded with Buck and Ball which is one full caliber lead ball followed by a handful of buckshot. Even if no vitals were hit, he was likely bleeding badly from several wounds. As any deer hunter can attest, a wounded buck can be tracked quite a way by following his blood trail, and the Spanish were likely employing Indian scouts as well.

Glass was determined to make it back to the little house at the bottom of the hill and into the arms of his loving wife, however, the Spanish commander detached a detail to run him down. By the time Andrew Glass stumbled back through the palisade gate he was likely near death from blood loss.

Perhaps his wife embraced him tenderly in her arms. However, frontier women, especially those betrothed to men like Glass, had to have a cold calculation about them or they would not long survive. In her mind, she would have quickly assessed the facts:
1. Her husband cannot be saved;
2. The chance of pursuit was likely;
3. His presence on the property, even as a dead man, might void her claim to the land.
Andrew Glass must disappear back into the mist from which he came.

Lightning-quick, her razor-sharp blade cut him from ear to ear. As the remaining blood drained from his brain, death was swift. The body was quickly dismembered—it is not much different from slaughtering a hog after all—and the slaves were called. Their instructions were clear. Perhaps she even made the point with the tip of the bloody knife:

Take each body part far out and bury it and don't tell me where!

The next morning the squad of Spanish soldiers pounded on the front door demanding Andrew Glass be handed over, dead or alive! A sweet young lady, freshly scrubbed and in a clean dressing gown—the bloody clothes from the night before were just ashes in the fireplace—came to the door. "Why, sir, I have no idea where Andrew is," she exclaimed, *and she was telling the truth!* Apparently, her plan worked.

About 30 years later a Methodist minister purchased most of Andrew Glass's original holding. His name was Newitt Vick, the founder of Vicksburg

We shall return to the house at the bottom of the hill shortly but first let us wander a few miles to the east!

THE CHAPEL IN THE WOODS
Chapter 3

On the edge of Vicksburg is a rural road named for an early place of worship. It winds several miles to the southeast, through a picturesque countryside that includes modest homes and churches, and terminates in a "T" intersection with Halls Ferry Road, just past a small Methodist church. The naming of roads in the nineteenth century was not a very creative process.

Roads were primitive, utilitarian things; no pavement, few bridges, no signs or mile markers. They were often just a trail through the woods, suitable for walking or riding a horse. Most of the early farms and plantations were along rivers and bayous. Later, as the interior of the county filled in, the roads were improved somewhat. They were widened and leveled enough to allow a farm wagon to pass. A team of mules hitched to a heavily laden wagon could not pull the steep hills in this region, therefore, roads often wound torturously along the ridge tops, as much as possible.

In the rainy season, winter and early spring, the roads in this area became a quagmire. Often times, wagon wheels would bury to the axle, so local commerce nearly ceased and overland travel was severely limited in the wet times. Most farms and plantations were nearly self-sufficient so this was not a huge inconvenience. In the spring as the roads dried out, mule-drawn graders would scrape the ruts from the road. Over the years the roads gradually sank into the ground, creating the sunken roads common to this area.

Waterways were unaffected by the rainy season; therefore, roads were largely an afterthought in this area during the nineteenth century. Hard paved roads did not become common in this area until the mid-twentieth century, but I digress.

Roads were local and named for where they went, thus Halls Ferry Road was the road to Mr. Hall's ferry across the Big Black River, and this road was named for the little chapel in the woods that it originally lead to. That little chapel, built by early settlers, is long gone but has been replaced by a modern, protestant church. Today, this pretty little country church is surrounded by one of the older cemeteries in the county. The small cemetery that surrounds this small country church is packed full. Some of the oldest graves now lie beneath the slab of the Fellowship Hall and pastor's office.

……………………………….

The protestant creed, particularly Methodism –founded by John Wesley, a former Anglican cleric who lived in Savannah Georgia—has deep roots in this part of the world. Many of the early settlers in this area were former British citizens from the colonial days and therefore protestant. During the American Revolution, Catholic Spain seized the area and for a number of years no open protestant worship was allowed. These men and women may have paid lip service to the Pope around Spanish officials, but in the privacy of their remote farms and settlements, they worshiped as they pleased.

When control of what was then known as the Old Natchez District passed to the U.S. in the late eighteenth century, protestant ministers began to arrive in earnest. One of the first was Tobias Gibson, who traveled from South Carolina to Nashville by horseback, then from Nashville to Cairo, Illinois, by canoe, and finally by flatboat to Natchez, arriving in 1799. He became a circuit preacher in the area from Woodville, Mississippi, in the south, all the way to the Walnut Hills—Vicksburg's predecessor—in the north, a distance of well over 100 miles. In his short tenure, this early nineteenth century Apostle Paul established over 60 churches.

In 1803 he contracted consumption, known today as tuberculosis. It is a disease of the lungs that has a gradual wasting effect on the body. In that day, it was untreatable—yet still he traveled. Twice he traveled over 500 miles up the Natchez Trace to Nashville to recruit more help. The Death Angel finally caught up with him just a few miles south of where one of his fellow ministers would found Vicksburg several years hence. In 1804, at his brother's home, on a ridge overlooking the Mississippi River, God called Tobias Gibson home.

Matthew 25:21 NJV His lord said unto him, Well done, thou good and faithful servant: thou hast been faithful over a few things, I will make thee ruler over many things: enter thou into the joy of thy lord.

In 1938, the body of Tobias Gibson and his grave marker were removed from his original burial place to the grounds of Crawford Street United Methodist Church in Vicksburg.

....

This brings us to the present and the recently retired minister of the modern church mentioned above. Uncle Raggy, as he is known to his YouTube subscribers, uses modern electronic media to spread his ministry much faster and wider than Tobias Gibson could have imagined. A while back, Uncle Raggy gave me a call about some mysterious manifestations that had been captured by his YouTube camera. In one video the dark shadow of a human figure can be seen sweeping across the frames of the video. Uncle Raggy did not experience anything unusual at the time, but on another video, he does. At first, he experienced a temperature drop. He confided to his viewers that there must be something wrong with the air conditioning. In a few minutes a guitar, sitting alone on a stand behind him, struck a note. At the same instant, a prayer bell on the opposite side of the room is struck. The change in his demeanor said it all. He was genuinely disturbed by the turn of events and quickly ended the video and exited the premises.

In our talk, Uncle Raggy admitted that on previous occasions strange things have occurred such as books flying across the room and unnatural noises being heard from the adjoining room. At one point he was sure someone had entered the adjoining office. Thinking it was perhaps a homeless person in need of shelter, he made a point of loudly saying he was leaving the office and wanted no trouble. Upon returning the next morning he found the room disturbed, but the outside door still locked. He also confessed that one of the previous pastors had left because of the activity. Were the original founders of the church checking up on him? **You never know when someone, or something, may be looking over your shoulder in Haunted Vicksburg!**

A VERY HAUNTED HOUSE
Chapter 4

The year was 1826. The City of Vicksburg had just been incorporated as a city the year before, and it had become a boomtown. Fortunes were being made and lost here, but it is not the gold or silver that drove the boomtowns of the Old West many years hence. Instead it was the fibrous bolls of *gossypium hirsutum*, better known as American long staple cotton, that is the "White Gold" of the Antebellum South. This shrub's fibrous product has been cultivated for cloth since prehistoric times but it is the invention of the cotton gin— short for engine—in 1793, by Eli Whitney, that makes cotton "King". Before Whitney's invention, separation of the fiber from the seed was labor-intensive and slow handwork. By 1826, the cotton gin had changed all that. Marketable quantities of seed-free cotton could be easily and quickly produced. Textile mills sprouted in New England, Great Britain, and France, fed by the fertile soils of the South.

By 1860, there were more millionaires per capita in Mississippi than any other state, but in 1826, the boom was just getting started. The Mississippi had become a thoroughly American River, with the land on both sides of the "Mighty Muddy" now part of the United States. Steamboats plied the river both upstream and down, and the Natchez Trace had fallen into disuse. Land was cheap and plentiful and slave labor was readily available. Slave markets existed in both Natchez and in New Orleans. If you cleared your land, made a crop, and covered all your expenses, in one year you were set. To this day the saying "I'm in high cotton" means life is good!

The owner of a local hotel, a gentleman by the name of George Washington Ball, a distant relative of the first president, was doing so well that he built a large two-story house that still stands today at the corner of Cherry and Main. A block away, a local builder had just completed another sizable two-story house with clapboard siding. The houses of Vicksburg were not yet the Greek Revival and Italianate mansions that would soon come to dominate architectural preferences as wealth increased. The house at the corner of Monroe and First East was styled like a Virginia farmhouse. The house was soon sold to Alexander Gallatin McNutt, a young Virginia lawyer. McNutt, who was later elected the twelfth Governor of Mississippi, in 1838, bought a large parcel of land, in conjunction with a partner. It was north of the city, not far from the old Spanish fort. He planted cotton and also added a new wing to his home to house his law office.

A nice house, a prosperous law practice, a promising plantation … what more could one have wanted? How about a beautiful wife? It just so happens that his partner had such a wife, and, as fate would have it, his partner soon took his leave of this life, allegedly at the hands of one of his slaves. Very soon thereafter, his dead partner's wife became his wife. (*There is something rotten in Denmark—or in this case Vicksburg—to paraphrase Hamlet*). The slave was quickly sentenced to die. As the hangman paused to give the man a chance to say his final words, McNutt struck up the band to drown out his remarks, and the condemned man swung mutely off into eternity. (What? You didn't know there used to be bands at executions? This was before the Internet and Reality TV. People had to find some way to amuse themselves).

Perhaps this was the beginning of the negative energy that has caused this house and property to be so haunted. At some point during McNutt's tenure in the house, a young niece became a member of the household. We do not know much about this little girl's life, only of her death. She was perhaps nine or ten in the 1830's when she became a victim of yellow fever and died, apparently while wearing her favorite blue dress. She still haunts the house and grounds. Numerous people have encountered her over the years; especially other children. Back in the 1990's, this house was a Montessori school and children took recess in the yard. When called in from play, a common complaint of the children was, "Why doesn't the little girl in the long blue dress have to come in?"

The Montessori school moved to another building many years ago. The house is now a bed and breakfast operated by Elvin and Pam McFerrin. When we first began the **Haunted Vicksburg Ghost Tour**, we sat down with Pam and Elvin and discussed the spirits of the place and at some point, we spoke of the little girl ghost. Pam asked me if I knew the little girl's name. I began to explain that there was little known of her; most details had been lost to history including her name. Pam stops me in mid-sentence saying, "I do!" She explained that when they first bought the place, their young niece and her family were visiting. As the adults sat and talked, Pam's young niece was running and playing all over the property. As the child came past, they asked her what she was doing. "Playing with my new friend," she replied. When quizzed, the little niece described the little girl in the long blue dress and concluded with, "Her name is

Maggie." *So, after 180 years of obscurity, we now know who she is… because she introduced herself.*

But Maggie is not the only spirit in McNutt House. A person of sensitivity—some might call them a psychic or a medium—once told me that as many as six spirits may be active in there. We do not have a lot of information about most of them. Some may have been slaves. We know slaves' quarters were on the property and bones have been dug up on the property more than once. One may be a man who committed suicide in a garage that once stood where the Montessori School Chapel now stands (recently renamed Maggie's Hall). Another is known only as Alice. She also introduced herself.

The first summer we were doing the **Haunted Vicksburg Ghost Walk** we had an elderly woman from Oklahoma City, probably in her mid-70s, who walked with a cane. I was a bit worried about her. It is a pretty long walk for somebody on a cane, but she had been keeping up pretty well. As we were exiting the property she suddenly stopped. Everyone else was already out on the street, so I doubled back and asked, *"Ma'am are you okay?"* She looked at me rather strangely and asked, *"Is there anybody here named Alice"?*

I answered, *"Not that I know of ma'am. Why?"* Her answer sent a chill down my spine … *"Because she's talking to me. I can hear her."* Okay, so now I am really concerned.

"Come on ma'am, let's get out to the Street and away from this spirit," I replied, but she said, *"No … no … it's okay. She's pulling away from me now."* After a minute she perked

up and was fine for the rest of the tour. I chalked this up to the strange things that sometimes happen in Haunted Vicksburg. A few months later, a friend of mine found a reference to Alice, who was among the third-generation of families who lived in his house… *Hello, Alice. It's nice to meet you!*

I am about to introduce you to the best known of the spirits that haunt the McNutt house. But before I do let me introduce you to someone who is very much alive…

I have a friend named David. He is, in a word, **flamboyant.** This young man lives life large. He is a skilled photographer and his Facebook page is full of beautiful photos of his lovely wife and step daughter. He has a taste for the macabre, and he is a paranormalist (aka a ghost hunter). He and a group of friends stalk the dark places, the old cemeteries, and the abandoned buildings with the same equipment you see on the television shows. David and his ghost hunters have done several all-night investigations of this property and on one such night they captured a black-and-white image of a man in uniform standing on the deck. The photo is so sharp it would be tempting to believe it was staged, but as you examine the photo from head to toe…there are no toes! The specter plays out about mid-calf and hovers in thin air.

We believe this is the spirit of a Confederate officer named David Weeks McGill, who is buried in the lower courtyard of the house, where his tombstone is still visible. David Weeks McGill was born to a wealthy South Louisiana planter family. In South Louisiana, sugarcane was the "White Gold". Sugar has been produced there since the mid-1700s. South

Louisiana is terribly hot, humid in the summer, and in the nineteenth century, an unhealthy place as well, with mosquito borne illnesses, such as malaria and yellow fever, common. Many wealthy planters and their families would retreat to more healthy and comfortable environs during the summer months. A popular retreat in the 1850's was Last Isle, a nineteenth century resort built on a barrier island just off the Louisiana coast. Here the Gulf breeze kept humidity and mosquitoes at bay. David's family was already on Last Isle in August of 1856. Young David was traveling with an uncle. Their plans were to join the rest of the family before the season ended, but rough weather inland had delayed their travel. David and his uncle's tardiness caused them to miss an appointment...**with destiny!**

The Last Isle Hurricane was first reported as a minimal hurricane near the Dry Tortugas on August 9th. As it raced across the warm waters of the Gulf it rapidly blossomed into a deadly storm. (Modern researchers believe it must have been at least a category 4.) Along its track it was encountered by schooners and steamers, but it would be forty-three years before a ship at sea could transmit a wireless warning to shore, and this racehorse of a storm would be ashore before any ship could return to port. Late on August 10th, it took a bead on Last Isle. A wall of water twelve feet tall swept over this low sandbar of an island, completely submerging it and cutting it in half. No one—in fact nothing—on the Island survived. David's parents and siblings were swept away along with everything else.

David went to live with his maternal grandmother and the uncle took a job on a Mississippi River steamboat. Sometime later his uncle fell into the river and drowned. Seven years passed and David grew to be a young adult. His grandparents sent him to one of the South's many military academies and, at the outbreak of war, he joined a heavy artillery battery stationed at Vicksburg. During the siege, a shell fired by a Union gunboat on the river mortally wounded him. He was brought to the McNutt House where he soon died. His men, fearing to risk death themselves, waited until nightfall, and buried him by candlelight on the grounds. **For, you see, death may be delayed but death is never cheated!**

There is a connection it seems between certain dates and spiritual activity. Halloween, of course, is the best known of these dates, and believe me, strange things happen around old Vicksburg late in October. But there are other dates as well. Days that may be specific to certain areas—and why not? Dates and anniversaries are important to the living, and if we believe, as many do, that these manifestations are the spirits or residual energies of those who once lived, why should dates not be important to them? One such date that seems of paranormal import to Vicksburg is July 4th.

Of course, many people are familiar with Vicksburg's most famous association with the national holiday that we now celebrate with fireworks and hotdogs. Independence Day is celebrated nationwide with parades and picnics and celebrations. Hearts are filled with pride, stomachs with good food, and streets with happy children. Vicksburg, too, was filled on July 4, 1863: its beds were filled with wounded and sick men, the fields around the city were filled with thousands of shallow graves, and the streets were filled with Union occupation troops as the siege ended with the city's surrender. For the first time in forty-seven days, the skies over Vicksburg were **not filled with fireworks** of a very real and deadly sort! There was not much to celebrate that July 4, 1863, but it was not the only July 4th with dark connections for Vicksburg. Allow me to explain.

The year was 1835. Vicksburg was a bustling river town. Mansions were beginning to sprout up around the city and cotton money was bringing a new respectability to the city. Vicksburg was really two cities. Atop the bluffs was Vicksburg proper, full of elegant ladies and courtly gentlemen. But down by the river was a coarser, rowdier part of town, filled with gambling houses, saloons and brothels, frequented by riverboat men and home to prostitutes and gamblers. Some just call it the Vicksburg Landing, but to most it is known as "The Kangaroo", an unofficial but widely used name. This nickname came from its most infamous house of ill repute.

There had long been an uneasy truce between the citizens of Vicksburg and the denizens of the Kangaroo. As long as their business stayed down by the river, most of the proper folks of Vicksburg would turn a blind eye to what was going on down there, but in 1835, a line was crossed. The Civil War was still twenty-six years in the future, and the patriotic people of Vicksburg were celebrating Independence Day with a barbecue on the courthouse square. Perhaps the smell of cooking meat wafted down the hill, for a gambler wandered up the hill to mingle with the crowd. It didn't take this rough man long to violate the moral sensibilities of the day. The attending "gentlemen" quickly dealt with the offending miscreant. He was unceremoniously escorted from the presence of the ladies, and a horsewhip was used to mete out some frontier justice.

Vicksburg was at a tipping point in its history. Barely sixteen years had passed since the city was only an idle daydream in the head of a Methodist minister from Virginia. It had been a rough and tumble frontier city, not too different in its demeanor than Dodge City will be nearly forty years in the future. The difference was Vicksburg had ambition! Antebellum gentlemen saw themselves as the American aristocracy. On the eastern seaboard, the older more established cities like Richmond, Charleston, and Savanna have the old families and sophistication to back that idea up. Young, rough Vicksburg had a lot of work to do!

It was decided the flogging of the immediate offender was not enough; the "den of iniquity" must be purged from the city. An ordinance was passed, and soon the Sheriff was posting bills around the Kangaroo. All gamblers were given twenty-four hours to vacate the city. Some did, but most simply holed up inside the Kangaroo, deciding to simply lay low until the wrath of the citizens of Vicksburg has passed. The people of Vicksburg, however, were not in a mood to forgive and forget so easily, and when no mass exodus of gamblers occurred, they put together a vigilance committee—this is the root from which the word vigilante sprouts.

In the 19th century, vigilance committees were not considered bad. In fact, they often mediated disputes, registered cattle brands, and performed other quasi-governmental functions in frontier areas. In the days before organized police forces, sheriffs also routinely used these committees to help them in times of need. (The old west posse was a type of vigilance committee.)

Doctor Hugh Bodley, a prominent citizen and by some accounts a Presbyterian minister—although this cannot be verified—lead the vigilance committee. As the posse descended the hill to enforce the ordinance, a shot was fired from the Kangaroo, and the good doctor Bodley fell dead. Who fired the fatal shot will forever be unknown, but the precise identity of the miscreant was immaterial, to the people of Vicksburg: **All the gamblers were guilty!**

The proper citizens of Vicksburg turned at once into an angry mob. Doors were battered down and gamblers were dragged into the street. Many were hung from nearby trees. They were, perhaps, the lucky ones, for the rest were subjected to a particularly brutal form of vigilante justice called tarring and feathering. Molten hot tar was applied to the bare skin, causing painful severe burns. The feathers were then applied, adding insult to injury. Those who survived were set adrift in the river. It appeared that brash young Vicksburg was not quite yet ready to enter the ranks of its older sisters to the east! This does however end Vicksburg's gambling problem for many years. In fact, it was not until 1992 that legalized gambling returned to the city on the hill!

On yet another **July 4th,** the darkness of the human soul welled up. The year was 1876. Thirteen years had passed since the end of the siege, and we were at the end of Reconstruction. The white citizens of Vicksburg, who saw their rights curtailed during the occupation, set out to retake Vicksburg from the Freedmen and the Carpetbaggers who had held political office throughout Reconstruction. A radical group of whites fired into a peaceful group of freedmen celebrating the holiday. No one was injured, but tensions continued to rise throughout the summer and fall as groups on both sides armed themselves. It culminated in a gunfight between black and white mobs on the Old Jackson Road that will leave twenty-nine Freedmen dead along this thoroughfare. The black community was traumatized and thus feared to claim the bodies, and **for the second time in less than two decades, unburied dead lay strewn around the fields of Vicksburg!**

Today Vicksburg once again celebrates Independence Day along with the rest of this proud country. The fireworks are harmless, the crowds are happy and music fills the air, but the spirits that still linger in the dark places remember that this was once a **Dark Holiday!**

TEARS OF THE PORTRAITS
Chapter 6

Located at 1010 First East Street, is an elegant Greek Revival mansion, now one of Vicksburg's premier bed and breakfasts and also a very fine restaurant. Its name, Anchuca, is a word from the Choctaw Indian language. It means happy home. Originally built in 1830, by a city official named J.W. Mauldin, the home underwent a major renovation in 1847, when Victor Wilson purchased it. He expanded the size of the house and added the Greek Revival façade it wears to this day. It was the first columned mansion in Vicksburg.

Wilson was a wealthy merchant who dealt not in cotton but in coal and ice. Cotton is a crop that quickly depletes soil. In botanical circles, it is known as a heavy feeder, quickly drawing nutrients from the soil. Soil conservation practices were not unknown in those days, but land was abundant, as well as cheap, and money flowed freely. Cotton was in essence the first industrial crop, and just as is often the case with modern CEO's, the bottom line was all that mattered to many planters. In about two seasons the cotton fields were worn-out and were typically abandoned; new land was cleared and planted. As the hardwood forest receded, good-quality firewood became harder to obtain.

Wilson saw an opportunity and began importing coal from mines in the north to heat the homes of Vicksburg during the brief but bitter southern winters. However, demand for coal dropped off sharply as the weather warmed in the spring, so, like any good businessman, Wilson diversified his portfolio and began providing ice during the warmer months. Ice was harvested from northern ponds and lakes in the dead of winter, brought down the river via steamboats, and stored in specially designed icehouses. So even in the heat of a southern summer, you could have ice for your Mint Julep, which was allegedly invented here in Vicksburg. Victor Wilson died in the summer of 1865, and his son-in-law took over the family business.

Anchuca next gave shelter to Joseph Davis, older brother of Jefferson Davis, the president of the Confederacy. Jeff Davis, just like Abraham Lincoln, was born in Kentucky, their birthplaces only 129 miles apart. Lincoln was born in February and Davis in June of the same year—history is full of strange coincidences. The Davis family moved to southwest Mississippi, today's Wilkinson County, when Jeff was quite young. In 1824, when Jeff was sixteen, his father, Samuel Davis, died, and Joseph, the eldest son, thirty-six at the time, took over the patriarchal duties of the family making sure young Jeff was properly educated in schools in Mississippi and Kentucky, then arranging an appointment to West Point. In 1835 Jefferson Davis moved to Warren County where he would later build his plantation, Brierfield, adjacent to Joseph's plantation, Hurricane. The U.S. Navy burned Joseph's plantation in 1862, and Joseph retreated to another plantation he owned east of Vicksburg.

Shortly after the end of the war Joseph took up residence in Anchuca. Charges of treason against Jeff Davis were dropped in 1869, and he returned to Vicksburg to visit Joseph who was near death. (He died in 1870.) Upon hearing that the favorite son of the Confederacy was back in town, the people of Vicksburg gathered in the street outside Anchuca. Finally, Jeff stepped out onto the balcony and briefly addressed them. This would be his last public speech. Jefferson Davis came full circle here in Vicksburg, having begun his political career here, by making his first public speech in 1843, just two blocks away on the courthouse square.

The circle of life is common to us all. We are born, grow to strength and maturity, decline, grow old and die. It is said that we're not really gone until the last one who remembers us is gone. **No one wants to be forgotten!**

The current owner of Anchuca related this story that happened to him a few summers ago.

While working in his office one day, he heard water dripping somewhere toward the front of the house. There are many things in an antebellum home that can be quickly and irreparably damaged by leaking water: Old, tinder-dry hardwood floors can be warped; 200-year-old plaster, often made with molasses and horse hair, is not easily repaired with the building products found at your local Home Depot; and priceless antiques of every description. So, he stopped what he was doing and went in search of this leak. He found water dripping from the middle of his dining room ceiling. That particular summer had been a very dry one; no rain had fallen in quite some time, so a leaking roof was quickly discounted. Climbing to the second floor, he entered the room directly above, looking around for any source of water. He discovered a small trickle running down the wall from the attic. He then climbed into the attic and made his way to the air conditioning units that had been retrofitted into the old house. Modern air conditioning units are always fitted with drip pans to collect any condensation that may make it past the collection pipes. But the drip pans were bone dry—this was not the source of the leak. The plumbing pipes were well away from this part of the house. He then made his way carefully across the rafters until he believed he was directly above the leak. He bent down and began to scoop the modern blown-in insulation from between the ancient timbers. Sweat beaded on his forehead. It was hard to see in the gloom of the attic. Soon his hands touched something hard, smooth, and rounded. He lifted two ornate antique portraits from the obscurity that had hidden them from the eyes of the world for decades. He was excited by his find; so excited, he momentarily forgot about the leak. He took the treasures back downstairs to his office, where he began to clean the antique bubble glass and the oval brass frames. A man and his wife, former owners of the home, stared back at him across the ages.

Once the portraits were properly cleaned, he knew just where to display them. He hung the images of his predecessors in the main hallway to greet the guests of the home, just as they would have in life, nearly a century before. As he hung the second portrait, the leak that had been steadily dripping water on the dining room table throughout his little expedition, suddenly stopped! Several years have passed since that day. The water stain still marks the dining room ceiling. No water source was ever located but the drip has never returned! **Perhaps it was the tears of the portraits that led to their discovery!**

A MAN OF FORTUNE AND MISFORTUNE
Chapter 7

*A common saying states: Lucky at cards, unlucky at love! It
implies that the Universe has a strange sort of balance to it.
In essence, if one is extremely fortunate in one direction
there must be a counterbalance of misfortune.*

Duff Green was a very wealthy and influential man in 19th
century Vicksburg, and like most wealthy men, he had a
home that reflected that wealth. Most of the notable houses
in Vicksburg proper in the antebellum period belonged to
merchants and businessmen. Plantations were out in the
agricultural hinterlands, although some particularly wealthy
planters also kept town homes as well. Duff Green did not
grow cotton himself. He was a broker, which is a go-
between, buying a planter's crop and reselling it to
merchants in New York, London and Paris, making a
handsome profit in the process. He married Mary Lake,
daughter of William Lake, a local lawyer and politician in the
early 1800s. His father-in-law made them a gift of the plot of
land at the corner of First East and Locust Streets, a
generous wedding present indeed. There, Duff Green built a
palatial Italianate mansion in 1856.

The Greens soon had a child, Annie, who was named for
Mary's mother. But the little girl succumbed to typhoid
before her sixth birthday. When the siege of Vicksburg
began, the Green's home was in close proximity to the river
and it made an inviting target for Union gunboats. The house
was struck several times by cannon fire from the river. To
save it, the Greens allowed the house to be used as a
hospital. Sick or wounded Union prisoners were housed on
the top floor as human shields, just in case the Union Navy
decided not to honor the yellow hospital flag flying from the

roof. Confederate sick and wounded were housed on the main floor. The Southern surgeons operated in the kitchen, located in the basement of the house.

Civil War medicine was quite primitive. Bleeding was still a common practice. It was believed that certain diseases came from contact with damp ground and "miasma", or bad air, was blamed for most others. Surgery was common, primarily amputation, but it was done in highly unsanitary conditions. Many an antebellum kitchen table still bears bloodstains and saw marks from the Civil War surgeons' gruesome work. Both chloroform and ether were very effective anesthetics and both were commonly used in the Civil War, but the siege lines around Vicksburg were tight, not even allowing medical supplies through. As the siege progressed amputations continued to be done, but without the benefit of anesthesia. Strong men were often used to hold the patient down while arms or legs were sawn off. The term "bite the bullet" comes from the Civil War, it is believed. A soft lead mini ball would often be placed between the patient's teeth so he would not bite his tongue off as a surgeon's bone saw cut off an arm or a leg. The mutilated projectiles, still bearing teeth marks, turn up from time to time. Amputated limbs were disposed of in a nearby room, the grisly waste eventually filling it from floor to ceiling.

The Greens took up residence in a large bomb shelter (commonly referred to as caves at the time) excavated in a nearby hill. Mrs. Green, once again great with child, delivered a baby boy, whom was named William Lake Green, but the nickname "Siege" attaches itself to the child and follows him throughout his brief life. Nineteen years later he was killed by a runaway wagon on the steep hill in front of this house. When the siege ended, Duff Green worked out a deal to allow convalescing Union soldiers to use the house.

After this, the family returned to the house where they remained until they died. But one more time misfortune visited the Green family, when their 23-year-old daughter, also named Annie, died from sepsis—blood poisoning—after scratching her scalp with a hat pin.

The house has many restless spirits. A ghostly Sentinel has been photographed on numerous occasions standing guard at the front steps. Guests have often reported seeing the apparition of a soldier sitting by the fire, grasping the stump of his amputated leg. A previous owners' granddaughter has reported playing with a little girl that no one else can see. Sometimes a child's ball can be heard bouncing down the stairs, and at other times, booted feet are heard climbing up those same steps. Perhaps one of the more lighthearted spirits is the one I call the "bathroom ghost".

The twentieth century was not kind to the antebellum mansions of Vicksburg. As the 19th century gave way to the 20[th,] wealthy Vicksburg settled into a middle-class life style and these vestiges of the "Cotton Kingdom" sank into disuse and decay. By the 1970's, you would have been hard pressed to recognize the former beauty of this home. The home's salvation came when a couple from south Florida bought the house in 1985. They soon began an extensive renovation, bringing this grand old lady back to the beauty of her youth. One hundred and twenty-nine years had passed between Duff Green's original construction and the 20th century resurrection of this mansion, and the things men considered essential had changed greatly. This mansion once hosted the most influential men and women of the Old South, but nobody would stay in the house today without the modern conveniences that we now deem necessities. Several bathrooms were added to the house during the renovation and perhaps the spirits of the earlier inhabitants found this new innovation fascinating.

When she resided in this home, the lady of the house had her own private bathroom, and she once confided in me that she always knew when something was out of place in it. One morning as she walked into her bathroom, she noticed that the toilet seat was down, and she distinctly remembered leaving it up the night before. I told her, the one thing we knew for certain, **it must've been a female ghost for no man would have bothered putting the lid down when he was through!**

As of this writing, a new owner has purchased this beautiful old lady and it is open to guests as a bed and breakfast, so that you can have the good fortune to experience the grandeur of the Old South!

Photo Section
(All Photos by Morgan Gates)

Danger lurked on the Natchez Trace

The McNutt House

Lt. Magill's Headstone

Monument to Dr. Bodley

The Balcony at Anchuca from which Jeff Davis spoke

The Duff Green Mansion

Steven Patterson's church, Christ Episcopal

A 13" mortar bomb – weight 220 pounds

One of many yellow fever victims at Vicksburg's Cedar Hill Cemetery

The Genella Building

THE LADY OF LAKEMONT
Chapter 8

In days past, men took the concept of honor quite seriously. Insults and slights, real or perceived, often led to violent retribution. Since ancient times, blood feuds or vendettas often consumed entire families or clans and could last for generations. The Hatfield and McCoy feud is probably the most famous modern example. Sometime in the Middle Ages, especially among landed nobility, the traditional warrior class, single combat began to replace the feud. Judicial combat, as it was known, came to be the accepted means of resolving disputes. At first, judicial combat among nobles had to be granted approval by the King—highly trained fighting men were too valuable a commodity to be squandered lightly. As the medieval knights morphed into the landed gentry of the late Middle Ages and Renaissance, the necessity of permission faded and the practice exploded. Broadswords and lances were replaced by rapiers and small swords. Dueling became more widespread, however, gentlemen were expected to be a "cut" above the common rabble. Dueling, though frequently deadly, followed a very formal pattern that had been outlined in several rulebooks. _The Code Duello_ is probably the most famous!

As America grew, dueling crossed the Atlantic and the caste restrictions eased. Pistols began to replace swords, especially in the United States. The pistol is a far more democratic dueling weapon, requiring neither years of practice nor the vigor of youth[3]. Southern planters, who saw themselves as American aristocracy, embraced dueling. The traditional weapon in the 19th Century incarnation of this

[3] Barbara Holland,_ A Gentleman's Blood: a History of Dueling_ (New York: Boomsbury Publishing 2003)

macabre practice was a smoothbore, single shot, muzzle loading pistol of large caliber. In fact, most well-heeled gentlemen would have owned an elaborately ornate boxed pair. The traditional range was 8 to 10 yards; however, both choice of weapons and range of engagement could vary widely if agreed to by both combatants. By the mid-19th Century, single combat was falling from favor as a means of settling personal disputes. The South was one of the last strongholds of this traditional custom, and even here it was technically against the law. Illegal or not, the tradition continued.

The gentlemen of the day were wealthy and politically connected, so many sheriffs of the day paid only lip service to the law by insisting that duels be held somewhere out of sight thus out of mind! In Vicksburg, as in many places along the Mississippi, sandbars became popular dueling spots. Across the river from Vicksburg, in Louisiana, lay large sandbars conveniently out of the jurisdiction of the local sheriff. William Lake (the father-in-law of Duff Green) was a lawyer and politician in early Vicksburg. Politics in the 19th Century could be rough-and-tumble affairs. Insults and violence were common. William Lake had given and received his fair share of challenges and had survived several duels.

In 1861, just after the start of the Civil War, but before it came to Vicksburg, William Lake was running for a seat in the Confederate Legislature. During the course of this campaign a challenge was issued, and Judge Lake prepared for what proved to be his last duel. He and his opponent, Colonel Henry Chambers, met on the west side of the river.

At this point in the narrative, there is some disagreement. According to local legend, the duel happened across the

River from Vicksburg and was witnessed by William's wife, Ann, from an observation deck atop their house. Some recent historians claim that the duel took place across the River from Memphis and Ann Lake was later notified of her husband's death. The gentlemen's choices in weapons were likely non-standard as well. Duels were often not well documented due to the illegal nature of the activity.

Each man brought a second—a good friend who was there to make sure the rules of *The Code Duello* were followed. Weapons were chosen; distances set at 40 paces ... then ready, aim, and fire. A cloud of smoke belched from the muzzle of both weapons temporarily obscuring the scene. When the smoke cleared, both men still stood. After the first shot was fired, the weapons were reloaded by the seconds and the distances again were stepped off. Once again, the crack of the report was heard and then the sulfurous smell of black powder. But again, neither man flinched. The leaden balls had once more failed to find their targets. The men needed to agree to a third shot, and both did so. Again, the weapons were loaded and the scene was again repeated. The Death Angel hovered nearby waiting to collect his due.

--Dueling pistols were deliberately less accurate than most weapons of the day and to practice with one was considered almost unsporting! For you see, the whole point of The Code Duello *was to decrease the likelihood of actual death! It was recognized at the time that the hot-blooded tempers and inflated pride of those who considered themselves superior had to have an "out". These arcane rules were designed to allow prideful men to vent their anger without completely depopulating the ranks of the so-called aristocracy. So, when the third shot also failed to draw blood, it was not an unheard of situation.*

Colonel Chambers and Judge Lake's seconds stepped forward and began to negotiate a peaceful end to the duel. *Apologies offered and reconciliation were not unheard of even after shots had been exchanged. There is nothing like the fear of death to throw a bucket of water on a fiery temper!* But that was not to be. Colonel Chambers took a decidedly ungentlemanly action—he fired a fourth shot while his opponent was unarmed and unprepared. This time, the lead ball pierced the breast of William Lake. Blood spurted from his chest; the wound was mortal. Judge Lake had but moments to live. His second cradled him in his arms as he died, his blood soaking into the sand of the muddy Mississippi.

Whether she witnessed her husband's demise or was later informed of it, Ann Lake's grief must have been overwhelming, consuming her throughout her life and maybe even into the afterlife: her restless spirit still wanders Lakemont to this day. Her distinctive floral scented perfume will suddenly become overwhelming both inside the house and on the grounds. The owners say the scent is often accompanied by the rustle of long skirts on the wooden floorboards. **Anne Lake still wanders Lakemont … waiting for her husband to come home!**

DEATH WEARS YELLOW
Chapter 9

With the modern advances in medicine that we have today, it is hard to believe that it was only a few generations back that the germ theory of medicine began to gain wide acceptance. Before this, disease was thought to be caused by everything from bad air to evil spirits. A simple scratch that you and I might ignore could go septic and cause death (see chapter 7) and there was no shortage of deadly diseases in days gone by. Smallpox, cholera, typhoid, diphtheria, tuberculosis, even the old childhood diseases of measles and mumps could prove deadly. Among the deadliest and most feared of the killers was Yellow Fever! This old killer of man went by many names. Yellow Jack, Black Jack and American Plague were a few of the more common labels for this mosquito transmitted, viral hemorrhagic fever. Its symptoms were high fever, excruciating back pain, and, in it's his later stages, internal bleeding. The disease would attack the internal organs, especially the liver, causing jaundice—yellow skin and eyes—thus the name. Dark bilious vomit was also common in the later stages—the black in Black Jack.

Yellow Fever is believed to have originated in sub-Saharan Africa[4] and to have been brought to the Americas with the slave trade. It might be called the slave's revenge, for it was seldom fatal to them. Here it found a vector in *aedes aeygpti*, commonly known as the striped house mosquito. This mosquito was also an African import. Normally, it is limited to tropical areas of the world, but the heat and humidity of Southern summers was close enough for this mosquito, and

[4] Sister Paulinus Oakes R.S.M. Angels of mercy a primary source Sister Ignatius Summer of the Civil War and Yellow Fever (Baltimore: Cathedral Foundation Press 2000) p43

its range expanded in the summer. One infected host would be bitten, and the proboscis of this little insect would act like a dirty hypodermic needle, spreading the virus to scores then hundreds then thousands. This terrible pestilence would burn through communities like wildfire, wiping out whole families, sometimes whole communities, until the cooler weather of fall caused this tropical pest to go dormant, and then the first frost of fall would finally kill the adult mosquitoes and break the chain of infection.

The rise of the steamboat and railroad transportation in the 19th Century allowed the disease to travel farther afield than ever before. Mortality was high in these pre-vaccine days. The disease was a summer plague, but it did not come every year. Often there was a decade or more between serious outbreaks. At other times epidemics were widespread and panic gripped the region.

Notable victims of "the Jack" were Newitt and Elizabeth Vick, founders of Vicksburg. They perished on the same day in 1819, 45 minutes apart. Had their son-in-law, John Lane, not carried out Vick's work, there might be no Vicksburg today.

In 1835 a dashing young officer of the US Army resigned his commission and married the daughter of his commanding officer, who did not approve of the match. He moved his bride to a plantation just south of Vicksburg. Three months later both husband and wife were sick with Yellow Fever. The young man eventually recovered but his wife did not. The young man's name was Jefferson Davis, the future president of the Confederacy. How history may have changed had he too not survived!

Vicksburg has had several infamous visits from this Yellow

Clad Grim Reaper. In 1839, the city was just over a decade old and struggling to rebuild from a large fire that swept through Main Street, consuming most of the timber structures of early Vicksburg, including the local volunteer firehouse at the corner of Main and Adams. The hapless firemen, with only antiquated methods to fight fire, were only able to save the cupola atop their own structure. It would be reinstalled on the top of Vicksburg's first city run firehouse, two blocks up the street, 31 years later. Much of the rest of the street is reduced to ash – including all the building materials collected by the congregation of Christ Episcopal Church to build their new sanctuary. The assembly, in existence since 1828, was undiminished in their resolve. The cotton money flowed freely and raw materials were abundant. The stockpile at the corner of Main and Locust was soon replenished and craftsmen were assembled from all over the region, when Yellow Fever swept through the town, killing most of the workers. The building was finally completed in 1843. It survived the war and is still in use today.

Vicksburg had a few years' respite from the American plague, but it returned with a vengeance in 1853! As has been the case throughout history, when people get scared they run! The town emptied out. People boarded steamboats, trains, and wagons.
Even walking, they fled the city, fleeing the contagion any and every way possible. There is some logic in flight, for the mosquito that spreads this disease does not range over large areas, but some of those fleeing are already bitten, and they took the disease with them to their supposed safe havens.

Not everybody ran. Significant numbers were already too sick to travel, and a few angels of mercy risked death and

57

stayed behind to tend to the sick and dying. One of these was the Reverend Steven Patterson, Rector of Christ Episcopal Church. This Godly man forsakes his own safety to attend to his flock and others in need, but eventually he too sickens and dies. With the coolness of fall, the grip of death loosens. Some of those infected survived, and the population returned. The dead were buried, including Steven Patterson, buried in the prayer garden behind his church beneath marble obelisk topped with a cross, **a fitting marker for a man who gave his own life in service to others!**

Yellow fever was not through with Vicksburg though; in fact, the worst was yet to come. We will return to this deadly disease later…

THE HOUSE AT THE BOTTOM OF THE HILL
Chapter 10

Let us return now to the little house at the bottom of the big hill. Time passed; the house was no longer deep in the wilderness. It was now just outside the city limits of Vicksburg. Vicksburg was a growing little river town, but the steamboat landing was on the northwest corner of town, and that is the area of town that was growing most rapidly. The southeast corner, which was the part of town closest to the house, was still sparsely populated. For this reason, this area became a waypoint for a great American tragedy.

In 1830, the US government passed the Indian Removal Act, thus beginning a tragic chapter in American history known as the **Trail of Tears**. It involved the removal, forcibly if necessary, of almost the entire Native American population of the Southeastern United States to a federally designated Indian Territory, in what is today Oklahoma. What many people do not realize is that there was not one Trail of Tears, but several. Vicksburg's part in this had to do with the Choctaw people. This Exodus in reverse was a logistical nightmare doomed to tragic results. Infrastructure was almost non-existent in those days. Roads were little more that trails through the woods nor were there yet any railroads. The first railroad in the Vicksburg area had been organized in 1831, but it would not be operational until 1840. Steamboats on the inland rivers were the only viable option for moving large numbers of people over great distances, and even that option was a poor one. In October 1831, 4,000 men, women and children began the long overland trek from their homelands in the eastern part of Mississippi to Vicksburg on the far western boundary of the state. At Vicksburg, they were supposed to board steamboats that would carry them on the next leg of their journey.

The trip from Vicksburg would involve going downriver over 100 miles to the mouth of the Red River and then upstream on the Red River to a point about 8 miles south of the modern location of Shreveport, in extreme west Louisiana. *This was the southern end of the Great Raft, a huge 180-mile-long natural log jam that marked the head of navigation on the Red River in those days (Captain Henry Shreve would clear the log jam in the mid 1830's. The city of Shreveport is named for him).* From there, they were to again travel overland to the Indian Territory.

The removal began too late in the season, and when they arrived in Vicksburg, the steamboats were not there and would not arrive until spring. There was little sympathy or even tolerance of Native Americans in those days, and the Choctaw were forced to camp outside the city in the area around the little house. Few provisions had been made for an extended stay at Vicksburg. There was not enough food and no adequate shelter for so many, and the winter that year was cold and wet. **Many died!**

You will recall that the first owner of the house was the highwayman, Andrew Glass. The second owner was a man with surname Howard, an early sheriff of the County. He built on a two-story, double gallery addition to the house in 1836. He had a beautiful young wife named Mary Elizabeth, who was only 14 years old when they wed. What is seen as shockingly young to our modern mind was quite common in days gone by. In the 19th Century life expectancy among white women in the United States, was much shorter than it is today. Health care was poor to non-existent. Infant mortality and death in childbirth were quite high, so men of means in their 30s would often marry teenage girls to ensure a good chance of siring enough children that at least a few would survive to adulthood.

From what we know, Sheriff Howard did indeed love his young bride. Soon she was pregnant with their first child, but contracted a postpartum infection. Childbed fever, as it was often known, was a bacterial infection that often went septic, usually resulting in death in the days before antibiotics. The irony here is that it was often transmitted to the patients by the doctor who delivered the baby, because they did not know to wash their hands before delivery. Mary Elizabeth lingered for several days before she succumbed to the malady. It is said Sheriff Howard walked the porch outside her room until her death. Even though Sheriff Howard did not die in the house, some portion of his spirit must remain. You can often hear the creaking of the floorboards as if he is still there pacing. Mary Elizabeth's spirit is still very much present in the house; she is the most active of the many spirits in the old house. More on Mary Elizabeth a little later, but first let me introduce you to a few more ghostly inhabitants of this accursed house.

This is not the same little house of our first visit in many ways. The hill is still there—Vicksburg Junior High School sits atop it now—as is the stream. The little house is no longer deep in the wilderness. In fact, it is almost in the middle of modern Vicksburg. Nor is it a little house anymore. After the Howard addition of 1836, John H. Bobb, a wealthy 19th Century gentleman, added another section in 1849. Mr. Bobb had a two-story Greek Revival section added to the front of the house. Life was good at the now big house at the base of the hill, at least for a while, but then came the Siege of Vicksburg. The house was a mile behind the Confederate fort guarding the railroad, and Union cannon that fired into the fort often overshot the works and their shells hit the house. It was struck numerous times, but it survived. After the surrender, Mr. Bobb was able to have the damage repaired.

Vicksburg was an occupied city from July 1863 until the end of the war, nearly 2 years later. Relations between the citizens of Vicksburg and the occupation troops were at times tense. One day in 1864, Bobb returned home to find a group of drunken soldiers in his garden. (John Bobb had beautiful gardens. In the 1830 census, he was listed as a florist although he had other business interests). Words were exchanged, the situation escalated, and Mr. Bobb struck one of the men with a brick. The men retreated but promised to return and exact retribution. John Bobb reported the incident immediately to the Union General Henry Slocum, the commander of the city, who promised to look into the matter and dismisses Bobb. When he returned home, the men, now armed, were waiting. Bobb was dragged down to the stream fronting his property and shot. His spirit is seen sometimes in the house and the smell of his cigars are common in the sitting room just off his bedroom.

The last owners of record before the house became a tour home were the Murray sisters. Their father had been a Union soldier stationed in Vicksburg, who fell in love with a local girl and stayed. The sisters inherited the house upon their parents' passing. They never married and grew more and more reclusive as they aged. The 80-acre plot on which the house stood during John H. Bobb's time shrunk to the just over an acre on which it now sits. The gardens once beautifully manicured grew wild to the point that the house could not be seen from the road and many people forgot it was there. Their only visitors were their doctor and some church ladies who brought them food. The house deteriorated near to the point of total ruin. Finally, the sisters' health began failing, eventually reaching the point where one of them died. The doctor took the surviving sister to a nursing home, where she too soon died. The sisters have now joined the retinue of spirits of this place.

The house was renovated and turned into a tour home. For years, there were no permanent residents, except the spirits, of course. With its convoluted and interesting history, it became a popular tourist attraction. Guided tours of the house were offered, and the spirits would often participate. Young Mary Elizabeth Howard was a particularly persistent spirit.

A popular story we tell on the **Haunted Vicksburg Ghost Walk** is that Mary Elizabeth would, from time to time, hijack a tour from the living guides, usually as they approached her room. Guests sent up the back stairway to the second floor would sometimes find themselves following a pretty young girl in a long brown dress. As they passed through the Howard section of the house and into the Bobb addition, they would find their young guide had mysteriously vanished. Moments later, their dumbfounded living tour guide, also dressed in antebellum clothes, would find them. **When they discovered that their upstairs guide was not among the living, the tour often abruptly ended!**

The house was closed, for almost a decade as the owner lived out of state. The vegetation once more closed in around it to the point that it could not be seen from the street. But the house was not empty … many of its former occupants continued walk the house and grounds, waiting for the next chapter in the story.

*Since this chapter was written the house has reopened as the McRaven House Tour Home. Tours are available daily,

but the new owners wisely do not live there, for there are already enough occupants in the house at the bottom of the hill!

"THE" RIVER
Chapter 11

There are two hundred fifty thousand rivers in the United States, many of them quite impressive with their own claims to fame, but only one deserves the title "Father of Waters"! The Native Americans called it this long before Hernando deSoto and his men saw it in the 1540's. Its name, Mississippi, is in fact an English corruption of a French corruption of a Native-American name that means "Father of All Waters". It is not the widest, the Amazon claims that title. It is not the longest, the Nile has it beat in that category. But for sheer impressiveness, it is second to none, and no river captures the human imagination like it does. Old Man River. The Big Muddy. It has many nicknames, but anywhere in this part of the world when someone says "The River" you know they are referring to the Mississippi.

To stand on an overlook near Vicksburg and gaze at the waters nearly 200 feet below, for a few moments you might be forgiven for thinking that "The River" is as unchanging as the mountains, but you would be very wrong. For in those few minutes you stand there, four and one half million gallons of water, each second, are passing beneath your feet. Water which fell as rain or snow in places as far away as southern Canada. Billions of cubic yards of soil are also suspended in that current, for "The River" gives as well as takes away.

The Mississippi is old, but not old like the Appalachians or the Rockies that define its drainage. The first Proto-River probably formed as the Western Interior Seaway began to drain at the end of the Cretaceous Period, and the river, in its more or less modern form, has been there at least 12,000 years. In many ways, it can be said to be alive, for it is not always easy to define life as it occurs in so many varieties on our little green planet. In general, most scientists agree that something can be called **alive** if it:

a. Has the capacity to grow
b. Can respond to stimuli
c. Can reproduce
d. Metabolize energy (eat)

In this most basic sense of the word, the Mississippi River is a living thing! It responds to the cycle of the seasons, the sun and rains. It eats—fields, forests and, in the past, even towns! In the spring, it grows—into a raging beast, which subsides in the summer. It reproduces, its offspring - hundreds of oxbow lakes and smaller rivers, like the Yazoo. It used to wander all over its valley but now it has been caged with concrete and steel.

The greatest Mississippi River flood in history occurred in 1927. That year, engorged on torrential spring rains, this beast of a river broke out of his older, less secure earthen cage—levees—and devoured 27,000 square miles of land, 246 human lives, and displaced thousands. In places the river was 60 miles wide and over 30 feet deep! It was 8 long months before the water receded. This catastrophic event led to the Flood Control Act of 1928.

The Mississippi River Commission was established and headquartered at Vicksburg. This branch of the U.S. Army Corps of Engineers was tasked with keeping the beast in his cage. Over the next few decades, the world's longest system of levees was built, floodways were established to drain away excess water, and a series of flood control reservoirs built to withhold water as needed.

In May 2011, the beast again reared up in anger. Engorged on record snowmelt, The River battered at the walls of his cage like an enraged elephant! The nation held its breath to see if the cage would hold. The bars bent but they did not break, and only limited damage occurred … **this time**! Even the most competent engineer will tell you it is only a matter of time. One day, despite our best efforts, this beast, THE River, will have his way!

In the 19th Century the Mississippi was still a wild river, but it was also a vital artery of commerce, so, despite the inherent dangers, people and goods traveled up and down the River. Countless towns sprang up along its course. Natchez was first in 1716, then New Orleans. Both Memphis and Vicksburg came on the scene in 1819. Flatboats, small one-way barges, and large log rafts dominated river commerce at first, then keel boats, narrow sharp—prowed vessels that could be laboriously and slowly poled upstream.

In 1811, "The New Orleans" was the first steamboat on the Mississippi. She was slow, heavy, and inefficient compared to her successors, but she was the opening of a new era. Steamboats would dominate river travel well into the 20th Century. The era of steam made travel more convenient but still hazards persisted and traveling the river was still a dangerous thing. Whirlpools and eddies were common. Banks could slough off with little warning. It was not unusual for a steamboat to leave one port, disappear around a bend, and never be seen again. Submerged tree trunks, called snags, lurked just beneath the surface, ready to rip the bottoms out of steamboats and throw passengers into the water and near certain death!

The River is a brutal psychopath, whose victims seldom escape. The currents are strong enough to pull even those wearing flotation devices under. Even today, any hapless worker, who is unlucky enough to fall into The River, might as well be falling from a 10-story building! Death is near certain.

The biggest danger steamboats faced were boiler explosions. Steamboats, as their name implies, were powered by steam. The steam was created in large cast iron boilers—the abilities to economically produce large quantities of steel did not come into widespread use until well after the Civil War. The pressure created by wood or coal fires would sometimes overcome the strength of the iron and they would fail with catastrophic results, literally blowing the ship apart. Red-hot coals, released from their metal enclosure by the explosion, would set wooden structures of the ship on fire. The most infamous of these mishaps was the final voyage of the steam ship Sultana, which departed Vicksburg on April 24, 1865.

Early in the war, both sides were using the traditional European system of parole and exchange, in which each man signs a written document agreeing not to take up arms until they are formally exchanged for an enemy parolee of equal rank. This system grew complex and difficult to manage and more difficult to enforce. After the fall of Vicksburg, the Union alleged that many of the Vicksburg defenders were back fighting within weeks, and the system breaks down. Prisons were established, in both the North and in the South, but by this time in the war, the Southern Nation was having trouble feeding its own people.

Conditions in Andersonville Prison, in Georgia—an open stockade encompassing some 26 acres and housing more than 30,000 Union prisoners—became appalling. Malnutrition, disease and exposure killed many. As the War drew to close, Union prisoners were sent to Vicksburg—now a Union base—for transport north and home. Captain Frederick Speed, of the Union Army, was in charge of arranging transport for these men and allowed 2,300 men to board the Sultana, a ship designed to hold a maximum of 376!

The Sultana had a leak in one of its boilers. Instead of having it replaced, as would have been prudent, the Captain ordered a patch welded over the leak. Heading upstream, fighting a strong spring current, the overloaded boat had to use higher than normal steam pressure to make headway. Two days later, just North of Memphis, at two o'clock in the morning, the boilers exploded and the ship was ripped apart. Anyone not thrown into the freezing floodwaters of the Mississippi was burned alive! Approximately 1,800 men died, making this the worst maritime disaster in American history. **Bodies washed down the river for weeks thereafter, some returning all the way to Vicksburg, 300 river miles south of where the explosion occurred!**

SEIGE!
Chapter 12

Fortress Vicksburg, the Gibraltar of the South, the High Tide of the Confederacy, and the Turning Point of the War … all these titles referred to Vicksburg during the war.

Early in the war, Abraham Lincoln said:

"See what a lot of land these fellows hold, of which Vicksburg is the key! The war can never be brought to a close until that key is in our pocket… We can take all the northern ports of the Confederacy and they can defy us from Vicksburg. I am acquainted with that region and know what I'm talking about, as valuable as New Orleans will be to us, Vicksburg will be more so".

The Union Military forces began to circle and jab at Vicksburg like a prizefighter circling a formidable opponent:

- In the spring of 1862 Flag Officer—later Admiral—David Farragut steamed up the River from New Orleans and demanded the surrender of the city. Not receiving the desired response, he shelled the city on and off for 67 days. Casualties were light. He had no significant ground forces with him and most of his guns could not be elevated high enough to be a real threat to the city 200 to 300 feet above the level of the river.
- Right before Christmas of 1862, William Tecumseh Sherman descended the Mississippi from Memphis with 30,000 men. The Battle of Chickasaw Bayou was fought for three days, just north of the present-day city limits, resulting in 1,776 casualties and a rare defeat for Sherman.

- In the winter and early spring of 1863, the swamps north and west of the city became an anthill of Union activity.
- Five months later, on April 16, 1863, Rear Admiral David Dixon Porter's flotilla of Union gunboats and transports ran by the Vicksburg batteries in the dead of the night, and a spectacular nighttime firefight ensued. The Union fleet fired indiscriminately into the city, leaving many waterfront homes holed by grapeshot and shrapnel.
- On April 30th, Grant's men crossed the River, 30 miles south of the city, and began fighting their way across west central Mississippi. The Battle of Port Gibson is fought on May 1st, Raymond on May 12th, Jackson on May 14th, Champion Hill on May 16th, and Big Black River Bridge on May 17th.
- On May 19, 1863, Sherman's 15th Corps—over 10,000 men—and part of Grant's Army of the Tennessee, attacked Vicksburg's works from the northeast and was repulsed. Almost 1,000 men were killed, wounded, or reported missing in this ill-fated afternoon battle.
- On May 22nd, Grant's entire army, over 32,000 men, attacked Vicksburg from the northeast, the east, and the southeast, along the Graveyard, Jackson, and Baldwin Ferry Roads. Again, the thrust was blunted. Grant realized that to overcome Vicksburg he must "out camp" his enemy, resorting to Siege Warfare! He sent word upriver for reinforcements, and his army grew from approximately 32,000 to over 70,000. As the ranks were filled, the cordon around Vicksburg tightened until the city is cut off from the outside world.

Siege is one of the oldest forms of warfare known to man. Sieges are mentioned in the Bible and in Classical

Mythology. The oldest siege that can be reliably dated was the Egyptian siege of Megiddo in 1457 BC. The longest siege of history was the siege of Canidia, present-day Crete, by the Ottoman Turks in the mid-1600s, which lasted 22 years. In American military history, the siege of Vicksburg is the second longest. Port Hudson, 150 miles south on the Mississippi River, held out for one more day. If you cannot overcome your enemy's defenses, starve him out. Vicksburg's 28,000+ defenders and 5,000 residents got hungrier, thirstier, sicker, and more dispirited as the siege progressed. Food was rationed. Confederate rations were never abundant amounts of food, but they were cut and cut again.

Men supplemented the rations whenever possible. Stock animals were the first to go. One diarist commented on the strange paucity of dogs and cats about the city. Toward the end of June, the men were subsisting on little more than a handful of peas or rice and, if they were lucky, a small slice of bacon each day. Soon Pemberton ordered the mules slaughtered. There is no record of cannibalism or outright death from starvation in Vicksburg, but many of those who died from wounds and disease were probably helped along by malnutrition. Some of those less dedicated to the Southern cause began to slip over the parapets in the middle of the night and surrender to the Union army.

The citizens of Vicksburg were doing little better than the garrison. A Vicksburg newspaper, printed on the back of a piece of wallpaper, listed only one item on the menu of a fine restaurant in town—"mule tail soup". By the end of the siege, large rats were the only meat available in the meat markets of Vicksburg.

Water was also in short supply, and temperatures in late

May and June can reach the mid-90s with near 100% humidity. Wells were not feasible in 19th Century Vicksburg. The water table was too deep due to the bluffs. The people instead used cisterns—large brick holding tanks excavated into the ground and fed from gutters that collected rainwater from the roofs. These held several thousand gallons each, but the supply was finite and could only be replenished with rainfall and there was only one significant rainfall during the siege. The thirsty garrison, in Vicksburg, drank from the numerous streams that flowed through the town until the Union Army fouled the headwaters with carcasses of dead mules and horses. The river was an inexhaustible supply of water, but rifled cannon mounted on the western bank fired on anyone seen moving around Vicksburg, so even river water was hard to come by. Soon water was rationed to a cup a day. The heat was unrelenting. The Confederate Forces were stretched so thinly they could not be rotated out, forcing them to live in the trenches where they sickened and died.

Vicksburg was surrounded by heavy artillery. From the river, Navy mortar barges launched 7,000 mortar shells into the city. The 13-inch mortar shell, weighing over 220 pounds, was made of cast iron, hollowed out, and filled with black powder. A burning fuse would ignite the powder and burst the iron case, showering huge ragged fragments across the city. They caused much damage, both physically and psychologically, for they moved so slowly that one could actually trace their path across the sky. Even at night, the burning fuse left a visible trace. Imagine watching these harbingers of death arc across the sky, wondering which one had your name on it.

The people of Vicksburg retreated into bomb shelters—caves they call them—dug into the side of the bluffs, but they are claustrophobic, dirty, and dark. They were mostly used at night. By day, many citizens chose to play a deadly game of tag. By watching and listening, they could determine if these deadly missiles were headed their way or toward another part of the city. Stress levels were high. Sleep was difficult, if not impossible.

Some of the churches were open but, even they, are not safe. At one point, the Union gunners observed people gathering at St. Paul's Catholic Church and opened fire on the building with long-range rifled cannon. W.W. Lord, the rector of Christ Episcopal Church, kept the doors open to anyone who wanted to come in and pray. His home, next door to the church, was destroyed when a mortar shell dropped through the roof and second floor, landing on his dining room table, seconds before his family was to sit down to dinner! His church still stood, pock-marked with shell holes, with all but one window blown out, and Rev. Lord's family took shelter in the basement. During a heavy period of bombardment, his four-year old daughter was crying hysterically in fear. Her mother comforted her by telling her, "Oh Dear, don't you know God will protect us?" to which the child replied, "Oh Mommy, I'm so afraid that God has been kilt, too."

Another story from the siege records the death of a small child. He and his mother were caught in the open by a fusillade of shellfire. The mother grabbed her son's hand and began running toward the shelter of their cave. After a nearby shell burst, she turned to discover she was holding just the bloody severed arm of her child, the rest having been torn away by the explosion.

The County Sheriff thought it cowardly to hide in a hole in the ground. He packed his family off to the caves but he himself continued to reside in his home. A Confederate regiment was using the lower floor as its headquarters, so Sheriff McRae was living upstairs. As he sat in the hallway reading, a shell fragment came through the window, penetrated his beard, and embedded itself in the bookcase. **His daughter, Lucy, recorded it in her diary as, "The day that Poppa almost died!"**

The aftermath of the siege left much damage and destruction around Vicksburg. There was hardly a house in town that was not battle scarred, and many had been completely destroyed. The dirt streets were full of craters the size of root cellars. Drunken Union soldiers, early in the occupation, torched a few buildings, but Grant quickly brought such rowdiness under control. It was perhaps a miracle the town was not completely leveled, considering the number of shells fired into the city. Poor fuses and the nature of the loess soil saved Vicksburg.

A British officer, "Henry Shrapnel", who subsequently lent his name to his product, invented the exploding shell in 1784. The British were the first to use this deadly device in 1804, at the battle of Fort New Amsterdam, in South America. By 1863, the use of exploding shells was common, most having a type of burning fuse that was *supposed* to burn at a predetermined rate. Cut to a certain length, it would, *ideally*, explode where you wanted it to, usually a few yards off the ground and directly over your enemy's heads! However, the point of detonation was as much luck as science. Often shells would explode too high in the air, causing a wonderful fireworks show but only minimal damage on the ground. Other times, shells would bury themselves deep in the ground. Often the heavy mortar shells would penetrate 20 feet into the light loess soil, where the earth would absorb most of the energy. Vicksburg was pockmarked and shell-shocked but largely still standing at the end of the siege.

Economically the surrender is good for Vicksburg. Unlike other Mississippi cities, first Greenville, then Jackson, and then Meridian, Vicksburg is not burned and left to wallow in the ashes. The "Key" is in Lincoln's pocket, and the Union Army intends to keep it there!

The city, and much of the surrounding countryside, became a Union enclave, deep in Rebel territory. Cotton was still king and the mills of the North were hungry for it. The plantations were put back in operation, the former slaves, or "Freedmen", were put back to work as contract laborers. In some cases, the plantations were under new management by Northern interest—"Carpetbaggers" they were called by Southerners. But, any of the citizens of Vicksburg, who were willing to sign the Union Loyalty Oath, were able to go right back into the cotton trade where they had made all their money before the war. Business is business after all! The money was flowing, security was restored, and postwar Vicksburg started to rebuild. Roads were repaired and houses were repaired or replaced.

Some whose houses were beyond repair choose to buy new lots outside the city limits and begin anew. Bound on the west by the Mississippi River, Vicksburg was, theoretically, free to expand north, east, and south. However, little growth occurs north and east. This was the direction of the fiercest fighting along the Graveyard, Jackson, and Baldwin Ferry Roads. This was land that had been soaked with the blood of men from both the North and the South. Land that, until recently, had been filled with shallow graves!

In 1866, the U.S. Burial Commission bought a large plot of land along the river, just north of Vicksburg, and began transforming it into a National Cemetery. A Herculean effort is made to locate all the hastily dug Union Graves and relocate the mortal remains to this "Bivouac of the Dead"! Southern ladies, led by Elizabeth Eggleston, set up a Confederate Cemetery within Vicksburg's Cedar Hill City

Cemetery and do likewise. Despite the best efforts of all involved, years have passed since the fighting ended and many graves have been lost.

Old-Timers around here report finding human skulls, washed down the hills into the creek bottoms, until well into the 20th Century!

I well remember this story related to me by a friend a number of years ago. In the early decades of the last Century, a relative of hers, an uncle I believe, was digging a cistern in the area where these battles were fought. As he dug, he unearthed a human arm bone with a mini ball embedded in it. He tossed it away and kept on digging.

The land to the north and east of the city remained thinly populated agricultural land until the Vicksburg National Military Park was established in 1899. The south side of Vicksburg, however, saw little action during the siege—only minor skirmishing, and no pitched battles. There were also a number of homes already located just south of the city limits. When the river shifted its course to south of town, in 1876, the decision was made: south is the way to go!

Not everyone abandoned the older parts of town, and the latter half of the 19th Century saw many new homes built in Vicksburg. Lazarus Baer and his young wife, Leona, were a prosperous couple who stayed. Their beautiful home, located on Grove Street, was built in 1870. The driving force behind this beautiful home was the lady of the house, Leona Baer. This young lady—she was 20 at the time the process began—was atypical for the era in which she lived. The late 1800s is typically known as the Victorian Era. It was a time when women are expected to be prim, proper, domestic, and subservient to their husbands in every way, but Leona was strong-willed, forward thinking, and not much bound by the customs of her day. She had some very definite ideas about her dream house and would tolerate very little compromise. She bought a burned-out shell of a house that had been destroyed by shellfire during the war. Literally, there was nothing left but four scorched brick walls when they purchased the property. She wanted an Eastlake Victorian mansion. The Eastlake style, named for Charles Locke Eastlake (1836-1906), an architect and designer who profoundly influenced popular taste in the decorative arts in the 1870s and '80s, came to us out of England, and in 1870, was quite new to the nation.

There were many fine craftsmen in the Vicksburg area, well versed in the building trade, but Eastlake was not a style with which they were familiar. A lesser person might have settled for a different architectural style, saved a few bucks, and still had a grand home, but not Leona! She had craftsmen brought in from the East Coast to build her house to her exact specifications.

The house had many features not common in this era, including a two-story indoor privy, an indoor plumbing system fed by a water tank in the attic, and an **indoor kitchen**.

Indoor kitchens were not common in grand homes of the 19th century. Kitchens were routinely built as outbuildings, away from the main house. The danger of fire was quite real in those days. Remember that 1830's fire on Main Street? By 1870, fire protection in Vicksburg had improved. Many of the fire stations now had horse drawn steam engines that could pump water from ponds, streams, and cisterns. One of these stations was the newly constructed Constitution Firehouse, and it lay only two blocks away from Leona's new home.

Leona thought the convenience of a kitchen under the same roof was worth the risk, with modern fire protection so close at hand, but her husband, Lazarus, did not agree and put his foot down! "No kitchen under my roof," he said, "and that is final!"

Like any good Victorian woman, Leona said, "Yes, dear," and the kitchen was built out back. Shortly thereafter, the kitchen mysteriously caught fire. The firemen from the station were just two blocks away and they came rushing around in their shiny new fire engine to put out the fire, but Leona was standing out front and refused to allow them to extinguish the flames. The kitchen burned to the ground—some people believe she set the fire herself. So, Leona got her wish, and the new kitchen was installed in the basement of the house. *Would you have told her no twice?*

Leona poured so much of her heart and soul into this house that we believe she is still hanging around watching over it… And why not? Paranormal investigators have long believed particularly beloved objects can absorb at least a portion of a person's spirit, so perhaps Leona is still watching over her dream home.

The house was purchased by a new owner in 2005. His vision was to turn the home into a bed and breakfast. Thus, began a long labor of love necessary to bring this house back from the brink of destruction. The 20th Century, especially the early years, were not kind to the grand old houses of Vicksburg. Cotton was dethroned by the boll weevil and globalization. The main course of the river shifted away from Vicksburg late in 19th Century, and first railroads, then later highways, made river transport less important.

Vicksburg, once the largest and most prosperous city in Mississippi, saw itself outstripped in both growth and prosperity early in the 20th Century. The mansions of Vicksburg, once show pieces of the wealthy elite, were now obsolete. They were old and drafty. With their high ceilings, they were hard to heat and harder to cool. In many cases, they were bereft of the modern conveniences that the smaller, more efficient, and affordable houses of the 20th century offered.

With the passing of the grandeur of the Old South, Vicksburg settled down to become a hard-working, middle-class city with middle-class values and needs. The old mansions were often cut up into apartments or converted to office buildings for doctors and lawyers. Some declined to the point where they became slums and were torn down to make way for more modern development. We lost many of these grand old ladies, and others were right on the brink. Beginning with Eva W. Davis' rescue of the Old Court House, attitudes began to change. People began to realize that these gems from a bygone era deserved to be saved and their history preserved.

The Baer house was luckier than many. It had remained a family home until mid-century and was a lawyer's office just prior to its rescue, so it was not overly abused. Still, the "blush was off the rose", and it was in need of work. The new owner set up a workshop down in the basement to begin the renovation, but the basement was where Leona located her kitchen, that she had fought so hard to bring within the house, and apparently, her spirit resented this intrusion!

The new owner started having problem with his tools. He would lay a tool down, turn away to do something else, and then when he returned, he would find it missing! The tool would turn up later, somewhere—somewhere he knew he did not leave it! This went on for some time. Eventually he moved his workshop from the basement and began the remodeling of the basement. This seemed to appease Leona, and his tools no longer disappeared.

The extensive renovations completed, the house opened as a bed-and-breakfast. The owner and his family once lived in China for a period of time, and they had a collection of Chinese antiques. So, they decided to use one particular room to display these antiques. Chinese antiques were not completely out of place in a 19th Century American home. Throughout the late 18th and early 19th centuries, the China trade was quite profitable. Both British and American merchants did business with China, primarily importing tea but also other trade goods, and Chinese antiques became fashionable among the wealthy of the day. This Chinese furnished room was to be called the Meling room.

This particular room was popular with the early **guests** of the home, but not so much with Leona! The original lady of the house, though, was not a mean spirit as some spirits can be—just a little mischievous. She played tricks, but never harmed. She expressed her displeasure with the decor chosen by the new owners by absconding with the glasses of guests who stay in the room. On many occasions, otherwise happy and satisfied guests of the house would have only one small complaint—they could not find their glasses when it came time to check out! Thorough searches conducted by both guests and host would prove fruitless, and twenty-two guests left the Baer House not seeing as well is when they checked in!

Finally, stumbling upon the reason for Leona's displeasure, the Chinese antiques were dispersed about the house and this room was re-furnished in American antiques. The glasses no longer disappear, but Leona has not disappeared. Every once in a while, she'll play a little trick, just to remind us that this was her house first!

Now Leona is not the only spirit that seems to have a fascination with eyewear. If you study paranormal phenomena long enough, you will begin to see certain patterns emerge. For some reason, eyewear seems to hold a fascination in the spirit world. My guests will often question why, but, of course, there is no good answer. I do have a theory though. For those of us who wear eyeglasses, this particular necessity is one of the most personal. In fact, we often euphemistically refer to them as our eyes! Perhaps it is simply the spirits' way of saying, "Look at me. I am here!"

The gentleman who restored this beautiful home has moved on and at the time of this writing the home is owned and operated by The Rickrodes, a couple which traded northern California for Historic Vicksburg. The home continues as a Bed and Breakfast, though they have given it their own touch. We approve, and apparently so does Leona, for she has remained largely quiet since they moved in, but she has played one or two tricks just to assure us that she is still there and to remind she is still watching!

THE CITY OF THE DEAD
Chapter 14

The first great American Yellow Fever epidemic occurred in Philadelphia in 1793. Dr. Benjamin Rush, a prominent physician of the day, mistakenly believed rotting coffee left on the docks of Philadelphia caused the disease. The disease came and went throughout the 18th and 19th centuries and it generally caused great panic among the people in the affected areas. Statistically you were much more likely to die of smallpox or malaria, which were endemic in the population in that day, but the imagination of man is much more agitated by dramatic casualties. Even today, thousands of people die in automobile accidents yearly. Most only make the local news broadcast, if it is a slow news day, but one plane crash, in which a hundred or more are killed or injured, makes national headlines.

The year was 1878. Radical Reconstruction had just ended two years before. Free blacks were facing a reign of terror that would effectively return them to a form of economic and political slavery for the better part of the next century. Once proud Mississippi, who boasted more millionaires per capita than any other state before the war, had become an economic cripple that will never fully recover. As if this were not enough trouble, Mother Nature was about to declare war on the people of the South. Far to the southwest, the Pacific Ocean, off the coast of South America, is warmer than normal. This cyclical phenomenon is known today as El Niño (*the child*) because it first appears around Christmas. Like a rock thrown into a placid pool, it sends ripples throughout the atmosphere.

In the southeastern United States, the normally dry late spring and summer was much wetter than normal. Standing water provided breeding grounds for an old nemesis, the striped house mosquito. "Fever Weather" it was called in those days. The armies were in position; all they needed to do is load their weapons. In Havana, Cuba, a small steamer named *Emily B. Solder* casts off her lines, weighed anchor, and set a course for the Port of New Orleans. According to her manifest she was carrying sugar, but, unknown even to her crew, she was also carrying a very deadly form of ammunition. She docked in New Orleans in late May 1878. The first casualty of the summer campaign was the ship's purser. His death was mistakenly reported as malarial fever, and next, the engineer was sick!

The first shots of this battle had been fired. Not far away the steamboat *John D. Porter* was docked. On July 18th, the Porter headed north. The disease quickly spread up and down the Mississippi River, infecting thousands. Vicksburg was five days, by steamboat, upriver from New Orleans. The *Vicksburg Herald,* one of the city's newspapers, reported when the disease first touched the ground at the steamboat landing:

July 23 – Thomas Murphy, 24 years, from the steamer John Porter, died in the Hill City Infirmary
July 24 – Henry N. Bryan, 24 years, died on board the steamer John Porter

On January 10, 1879, after the epidemic had run its course, the *Vicksburg Herald* attempted to catalogue the deaths throughout the summer and early fall.[5] The information available on the first victims was somewhat detailed, almost a truncated obituary, but as the epidemic progressed and the death rate mounted, little more than a list of names,

---

[5] Vicksburg Herald Jan, 10 1879 - Transcribed by Janice Rice- for Genealogy Trails

sometimes not even full names, was all that could be published. Here is the progression of the epidemic:

July 25 – one death   August 1 – one death
August 9 – one death   August 10 – one death
August 11 – one death   August 17 – two deaths
August 18 – one death   August 19 – six deaths
August 20 – eight deaths August 21 – 22 deaths
August 22 – 13 deaths   August 23 – 12 deaths
August 24 – 64 deaths   August 27 – 22 deaths
August 28 – 17 deaths   August 29 – 16 deaths
August 31 – 25 deaths   September 1 – 20 deaths
September 2 – 20 deaths September 3 – 43 deaths

295 names were listed in the *Herald's* compilation, but we know there were many more. In the 1870s hospitals generally served only the indigent. Doctors still made house calls in those days, and people of means tended to have the doctor come to them. This can be confirmed by the number of names on tombstones of prominent citizens that were interred at Vicksburg's Cedar Hill Cemetery that were not put on this list. Also, many more would have died quietly at home without any sort of medical treatment at all. In truth, nobody really knows how many people died during this time. Some reliable sources estimate the death rate as high as 25% of the population. If that is true, then this epidemic had a similar mortality rate to the Black Plague of the Middle Ages. Probably between 1,000-2,000 people died in and around Vicksburg, in 1878, during this epidemic. Many more would have sickened. Of those, some would recover completely after weeks of convalescence. Others would remain in a debilitated state for the rest of their lives.

Allow me to digress a moment, for we must back up a few

years to introduce a group of ladies that became key players in Vicksburg's survival and recovery: The Catholic order of nuns known as the Sisters of Mercy. The Sisters arrived in Vicksburg in 1860 from Baltimore, Maryland, to establish a school. The Catholic Diocese purchased a three-story house on Crawford Street, and on October 19, 1860, the Sisters took possession. Less than three months later, Mississippi would be the second state to secede from the Union, and four months after that, the Civil War would begin.

Vicksburg was a relatively peaceful place for the first year of the war, but in May, 1862, David G. Farragut bombarded the city from the River for 67 days. Shortly thereafter the Sisters evacuated the city. Soon they were working at the Confederate hospital at Mississippi Springs, about 30 miles southeast of Vicksburg. They followed the hospital to Jackson, and finally into Alabama. In May, 1864, nearly a year since the city surrendered, the Sisters returned to reopen the school. Union General Henry Slocum, who was the commander of the city, had taken their house on Crawford Street for his own use and declined the Sisters' petition for return of their property. But the Sisters still had connections up north. Some weeks later, the Secretary of War himself wrote to General Slocum, ordering him to vacate the house[6].

In the late summer and early fall of 1878, the Sisters of Mercy were involved in warfare against a foe of a very different sort. As the fever raged through Vicksburg, the primitive medical facilities of the day were overwhelmed. The doctors and nurses could not even protect themselves from this deadly fever. Dr. David Booth, the physician in charge of the city hospital, feeling that he, too, had been

---

[6] Sister Paulinus Oakes R.S.M.Angels of mercy a primary source Sister Ignatius Summer of the Civil War and Yellow Fever (Baltimore: Cathedral Foundation Press 2000) p43

infected, turned the hospital over to the Sisters. Dr. Booth himself succumbed to the disease later that summer. With the coming of fall, the fever's grip on the city loosened. Finally, in November, their school reopened with a much-reduced enrollment. One of the Sisters wrote:

"The moon looks down, so lustrous, yet so coldly, upon the city of the dead. Houses are closed, stores vacated, and besides ourselves and the physicians, scarcely a creature to be seen ..."[7]

The Sisters would remain in the medical profession around Vicksburg until 1991.

In 1901, Walter Reed, a US Army physician, led a team that, once and for all, confirms the link between the striped house mosquito and Yellow Fever. Mosquito Eradication Programs allowed the first effective methods of controlling this deadly disease. In 1937, the first effective vaccine is invented.[8] The Yellow Clad Grim Reaper still exists in the world. He still swings his scythe in the impoverished tropical backwaters of the world, *but the word **fever** no longer inspires terror in the hearts of the Southern people!*

---

[7] Ibid (Oakes)

[8] Molly Caldwell Crosby, American Plague; the Untold Story of Yellow Fever (New York: Berkley books)

Vicksburg was built on a series of high bluffs overlooking the Mississippi River. This natural geography was the reason the city was founded in the first place, the reason the Confederate Army fortified the city, and, of course, the reason the Union Army besieged the city.[9] Especially in the older parts of the city, this geography is most obvious, so when I give directions to people who are new to the city, I tell them that Vicksburg is three-dimensional—you can go left and right, up and down, and while it may be easy to confuse left and right, it is hard to confuse up and down. Often my directions might be: "…go to the corner and go up the hill two blocks."

On the north end of Washington Street, about three blocks from the bottom of the hill, where the Kangaroo used to be, stands an old red brick building that dates back to the 1830s. It is perhaps the oldest building left standing on Washington Street. The building is beautiful, not in the ornate way of an Italianate mansion, but in its straightforward simplicity of form and function. It is made of locally fired clay bricks and likely constructed by skilled slave labor. Down in the basement, the building's bones lay exposed. The brick wall expands the further it goes down. The very base is over 10 feet wide, distributing the weight into the soil and allowing the multi-layer brick wall to extend four stories up. Brick arches distribute the weight and allow openings large enough that the old freight wagons could pass through. There used to be passageways connecting to underground tunnels, the old sewers of the city, and to the basement of

---

[9] Warren Graubeau, Ninety Eight Days a geographers view of the Vicksburg Campaign (Knoxville: the University of Tennessee Press 2000)

adjacent buildings. Although closed up, you can still see the outline of the entrances in the brick. Huge cypress beams cut from the forest primeval, nearly 200 years ago, support the floors above. You can still see where somebody carved their name in one of these massive timbers and dated it 1920. Some folks around here still refer to this old building as the Genella building. The Bonelli Brothers, Italian immigrants, ran a dry goods store here for many years in the early 20th Century. Their name is still visible on the iron doorstep at the front of the building.

This old building has a history that stretches back to the early days of Vicksburg. The rear of the building took hits from the Union gunboats during the siege. The extensive repairs made to the badly damaged walls are still in evidence near the back basement door. In the late 19th Century this building was home to a dance hall. "The Palace" was its name. You know what a dance hall is—it is the same thing as an Old West Saloon. Dance halls were popular in the 19th Century. They arose first in the working-class neighborhoods of Paris in the 1830s. They usually involved raucous music and dancing girls mixed with the consumption of alcohol.

The saloon was an Americanized version. These were not exclusive to the West, but were common in many 19th Century cities. This building was such a place. It was a place where a rider, weary from the dusty trail, or a river boatman from one of the steamboats, could get a drink, unwind and be entertained. The saloon occupied the first floor, the second floor was the dance hall with the pretty ladies, and the third floor was, *allegedly,* a brothel, and like many such places, it harbors a dark energy. An 1890 edition of the Vicksburg Newspaper caries the account of a cold-blooded murder there, but who knows how many other vile misdeeds went unreported.

More recently, up until the fall of 2011, the building was an eclectic little antique shop called River Chicks and was operated by a friend of ours, Dianna. She lived alone in a small apartment in the back and was a first-hand witness to the haunted nature of the building. Shortly after the business opened, Dianna began to suspect that the building was active. In the fall of 2010, she allowed a local Ghost Hunting Group to do an all-night investigation. The primary evidence gathered that night was in the form of EVPs. An EVP, or electronic voice phenomenon, is an auditory manifestation often gathered during paranormal investigations. As researchers explore a location believe to be haunted, they will talk to, ask questions of, and even try to provoke the spirits to get a reply. A small digital voice recorder will be used to record any reply. At the end of the investigation, the recording will be downloaded and, using a special computer program, the response, if any, can be amplified and clarified. Sometimes a human voice can be identified. These are the EVPs.

Over 40 electronic voice phenomena were identified that night. Some were obviously the ladies of the evening who once worked there, for they were vulgar and coarse. In response to the question "Do you work here?", a male voice responded, "We all work here!" A child's voice says over and over, "Hello, hello." The owner of the shop had often heard this little girl's voice, audibly, both before and after the investigation. At one point she responded to it but was met with only "dead" silence. The most heart wrenching of the responses recorded was also a little girl's voice. It plaintively calls out, "I'm still alive down here." I've heard this EVP with my own ears. It is a clear and distinct human voice. I've often wondered at its source.

There seem to be many children's ghosts about Vicksburg. Some paranormalists theorize that spirits of the very young are easily confused and get lost. In the basement of the building there once was a cistern—underground water storage—which was filled in decades ago. Did this child die by falling into the water-filled pit? We will likely never know for certain.

Have you ever watched one of those nature documentaries where the cameramen set up and film for several days and, after a few days, the wild animals began to ignore the camera and go about their daily routine? So, it was in the Genella building, for the paranormal world began to open up after the investigation.

One day a woman entered the shop. After a few minutes walking, around she identified herself as a medium from the New York area. She then proceeded to tell Diana she had no need to fear a break-in or a robbery while she was in the building for there was a male spirit there that had taken a liking to her. Diana confidentially admitted that she always felt protected in the building. One day, as a powerful thunderstorm was rolling across the river, she heard a male voice over her shoulder saying, "Don't be afraid." At the time, she was alone in the building!

River Chicks became a part of our tours for almost a year, and we had quite a few interesting encounters in that building. One night, a lady on the tour could distinctly hear a piano playing. In the week leading up to July 4th, (see Chapter 5) during one of our tours, a small wooden carving literally leapt from a shelf and landed at a young lady's feet. I picked it up and put it back on the shelf, and, once more, it leapt from the shelf, landing in the exact same spot. This time, when I picked it up, I placed it not back on the shelf but on a desk halfway across the room. As we moved on to the second floor, the same young lady refused to enter the old dance hall. She said she had a strange feeling about it. As she stood alone in the hallway, she watched as the door to the empty apartment in the back of the building opened and closed, all by itself. We found her waiting on the street, still quite shaken.

In the late summer of 2011, Diana got a call from some friends in another state. They offered her a good job—much too good of a job to turn down. I told her that we would certainly miss her, but the spirits of this building would miss her even more. Over the next several weeks, strange noises were heard about the building—noises she had never heard in the over two years that she had lived there. Doors slammed all over the building when there was nobody inside but her. A few days before she left, she called me. She had been up in her laundry room on the second floor when, from the empty apartment behind her, she heard strange noises. Stepping out into the hall to investigate, she found the door to the vacant apartment standing open. Just then, a full body apparition appeared in the doorway. It looked right at her, then turned, and walked away! I guess it just came to say goodbye!

CONCLUSION

We hope you have enjoyed our little compilation of history, mystery, and more. We have but scratched the surface of the rich history of this area. We invite you to visit us. The Vicksburg National Military Park and the Old Court House Museum are open daily, and they alone are worth the trip. Each spring Vicksburg's annual tour of homes, known as The Vicksburg Pilgrimage, opens the doors to numerous historic homes. Fine dining and elegant lodging abound. We invite you to come explore.

While you are here, be sure to book a ghost tour and take a *walk on the dark side*. Our Ghost Walk takes you through the oldest neighborhood in Vicksburg. Our Ghostly Driving Tour includes stops in four different historic parts of town and entrance into Miss Leona's house. We offer various historic tours around the city as well! Bring comfortable shoes, a sense of adventure, and your camera. Be prepared, for "strange things happen in Haunted Vicksburg," and be on the lookout for out next book in the Rediscovering Historic Vicksburg series!

For more information go to www.hauntedvicksburg.com

ACKNOWLEDGMENTS

It would be Impossible to acknowledge everyone and every source from which the information in this book has been drawn, for I have been collecting these tidbits of information for over 30 years. I have read hundreds of books and articles, and talked to thousands of people, many of whose names I do not remember. Where I have taken a quote or a number from a source, I have credited it if possible. If you do much reading on history, you will discover that different authors will have differing opinions, and may even quote contradictory "facts". Even with something as well documented as the Civil War, you will discover that not everything is known, and there are sometimes widely varying interpretations. In my own personal experience in working with people over many decades, I have discovered that on controversial subjects, if you take the two most extreme interpretations and split the difference, you will usually be fairly close to the truth! Of course, the further back in time you go, the fuzzier the facts get.

In a Ghost Tour, you also deal with Oral Traditions, or Folklore. This, of course, was man's first way of recording history, and is still widely used to this day. Folklore is even more subject to differing interpretations and embellishment than written history, but usually there is at least a kernel of truth there, if you know how to look for it. In some places, I have used folklore to fill in the gaps in the history and, in others, I have used history from similar events to add veracity to the folklore. In these cases, I am satisfied that I have given you, the reader, an acceptable and reasonable story that is as close the truth as possible.

Special thanks to the following organizations & individuals:

The Vicksburg Guide Association

The Delta Paranormal Project

Mississippi Paranormal Research Institute

Joyce Hughes – retired tour guide at McRaven tour home

Joyce Hill – Licensed Guide VNMP, former McRaven tour guide

Elvin & Pam McFerrin owners of McNutt House

Harry & Alicia Sharpe

Last, but not least, thanks to my "partner in time", Meshea Crysup. Without her help, this book would have forever been just a file on my computer.